MORE SUPER SIMPLE SCIENCE

SCIENCE EXPERIMENTS WITH

GRAVITY & MOTION

A Division of ABDO
ABDO
Publishing Company

BY ALEX KUSKOWSKI   Consulting Editor, Diane Craig, M.A./Reading Specialist

visit us at www.abdopublishing.com

Published by ABDO Publishing Company, a division of ABDO, P.O. Box 398166, Minneapolis, Minnesota 55439. Copyright © 2014 by Abdo Consulting Group, Inc. International copyrights reserved in all countries. No part of this book may be reproduced in any form without written permission from the publisher. Super SandCastle™ is a trademark and logo of ABDO Publishing Company.

Printed in the United States of America, North Mankato, Minnesota
062013
112013

PRINTED ON RECYCLED PAPER

Editor: Liz Salzmann
Content Developer: Alex Kuskowski
Cover and Interior Design and Production: Mighty Media, Inc.
Photo Credits: Aaron DeYoe, Shutterstock

The following manufacturers/names appearing in this book are trademarks:
DecoArt® Americana®, Crystal Sugar®, Pelouze®, Pyrex®, Walking Shop™ by Sportline®

Library of Congress Cataloging-in-Publication Data
Kuskowski, Alex.
  Science Experiments with gravity & motion / by Alex Kuskowski ; consulting editor, Diane Craig.
    p. cm. -- (More super simple science)
  Audience: 005-010.
  ISBN 978-1-61783-850-7
1. Gravity--Experiments--Juvenile literature. 2. Motion--Experiments--Juvenile literature. 3. Momentum (Mechanics)--Experiments--Juvenile literature. 4. Science--Methodology--Juvenile literature. I. Craig, Diane. II. Title. III. Title: Science experiments with gravity and motion.
  QC178.K975 2014
  531.078--dc23
                      2012049954

Super SandCastle™ books are created by a team of professional educators, reading specialists, and content developers around five essential components—phonemic awareness, phonics, vocabulary, text comprehension, and fluency—to assist young readers as they develop reading skills and strategies and increase their general knowledge. All books are written, reviewed, and leveled for guided reading, early reading intervention, and Accelerated Reader® programs for use in shared, guided, and independent reading and writing activities to support a balanced approach to literacy instruction.

TO ADULT HELPERS

Learning about science is fun and simple to do. There are just a few things to remember to keep kids safe. Be sure to review the activities before starting and be ready to assist your budding scientist when necessary.

TABLE OF CONTENTS

You can be a scientist! It's super simple. Science is all around you. Learning about the world around you is part of the fun of science. Science is in your house, your backyard, and on the playground.

Find science with marbles and rulers. Look for science in clay and rice. Try the activities in this book. You'll never know where to find science unless you look!

SCIENCE WITH GRAVITY & MOTION

Learn about science with gravity and motion. Gravity is the reason things fall down when you drop them. In this book you will see how gravity and motion can help you learn about science.

WORK LIKE A SCIENTIST

Scientists have a special way of working. It is a series of steps called the Scientific Method. Follow the steps to work like a scientist.

1. Look at something. What do you see? What does it do?

2. Think of a question about the thing you are watching. What is it like? Why is it like that? How did it get that way?

3. Think of a possible answer to the question.

4. Do a test to find out if you are right. Write down what happened.

5. Think about it. Were you right? Why or why not?

KEEP TRACK

There's another way to be just like a scientist. Scientists make notes about everything they do. So get a notebook. When you do an experiment, write down what happens in each step. It's super simple!

WHAT YOU WILL NEED

balloon

books

card stock

chair

clay

clear tape

cutting board

drinking glass

drinking straw

duct tape

flat glass marble

funnel

hole punch

jar with lid

large plastic tub

liquid soap

marbles

measuring cups & spoons

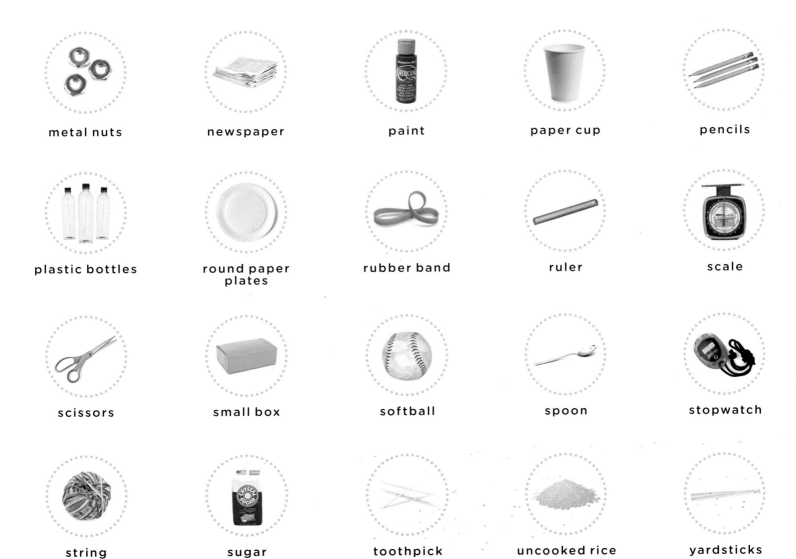

metal nuts

newspaper

paint

paper cup

pencils

plastic bottles

round paper plates

rubber band

ruler

scale

scissors

small box

softball

spoon

stopwatch

string

sugar

toothpick

uncooked rice

yardsticks

MAJOR MARBLE MOMENTUM

WHAT YOU WILL NEED

2 yardsticks

ruler

duct tape

6 marbles

DIRECTIONS

1. Lay the yardsticks on a flat surface. Line them up 1 inch (2.5 cm) apart. Tape them in place.

2. Put four marbles between the yardsticks. Make sure they touch each other.

3. Roll one marble toward the line of marbles. Watch it hit the marbles. The marble on the opposite end moves!

4. Try rolling two marbles instead of one. Roll them together at the same time. Watch them hit the other marbles. What happens this time?

WHAT'S GOING ON?

A moving marble has **momentum**. When it hits the other marbles, the momentum passes from one to the next. Two marbles have more momentum than one. They make two marbles move.

GOOFY GRAVITY EXPERIMENT

WHAT YOU WILL NEED

scale

softball

marble

book

paper

DIRECTIONS PART 1

1. Weigh the softball. Weigh the marble. Which one is heavier?

2. Hold the marble in one hand and the softball in the other. Keep your hands at the same height.

3. Drop both objects at the same time. What happens?

WHAT'S GOING ON?

Gravity pulls objects down at the same speed. Weight doesn't matter. The softball was heavier. But both objects hit the ground at the same time.

DIRECTIONS PART 2

④ Repeat Part 1 with a flat sheet of paper and a book. What happens this time?

⑤ **Crumple** the paper into a ball.

⑥ Hold the paper ball in one hand and the book in the other. Drop them at the same time. What happens this time?

WHAT'S GOING ON?

Air can change how gravity works. The flat paper is thin. The air pushes it up as it falls. This slows it down. The air doesn't affect the ball of paper the same way. It falls at the same speed as the book.

VERY PECULIAR PENDULUMS

WHAT YOU WILL NEED

string

ruler

scissors

22 metal nuts

2 pencils

clear tape

chair

stopwatch

paper

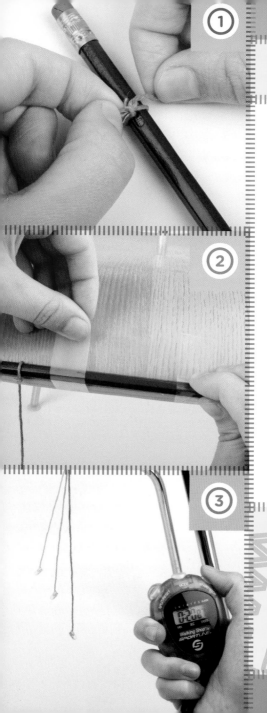

DIRECTIONS PART 1

① Cut one string 12 inches (30 cm) long. Cut another string 6 inches (15 cm) long. Tie one end of each string to a metal nut. Tie the other ends to pencils.

② Tape the pencil with the long string along the edge of a chair. The string should hang down. Hold the long string straight out. Let go and start the stopwatch. Count the number of times it swings back and forth in 30 seconds. Write down the number.

③ Repeat step 2 with the short string.

DIRECTIONS PART 2

④ Untie the strings from the pencils. Thread ten nuts onto each string. Tie the strings to the pencils again.

⑤ Tape the pencil with the long string along the edge of a chair like before. Hold the long string straight out. Let go and start the stopwatch. Count the number of times it swings back and forth in 30 seconds. Write down the number.

⑥ Repeat step 5 with the short string.

7 Compare the number of swings in Part 1 and Part 2. What was different? What was the same?

WHAT'S GOING ON?

The strings are **pendulums**. The length of the strings affects how fast each pendulum swings. The shorter the string, the faster it swings. The weight on the strings doesn't affect how they swing.

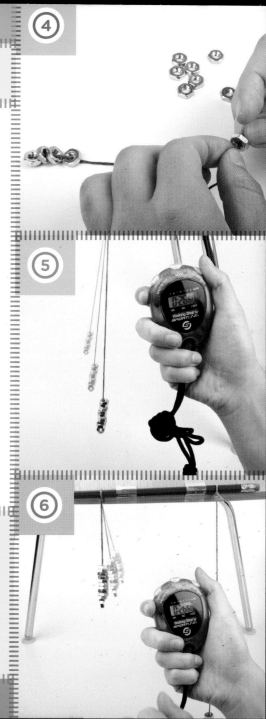

04 MAGNIFICENT ROLLING MARBLES

WHAT YOU WILL NEED

newspapers

paint

paper cup

marble

spoon

2 round paper plates

scissors

DIRECTIONS

1 Cover your work surface with newspaper. Put some paint in a paper cup.

2 Drop the marble in the paint. Use a spoon to put the marble on a paper plate. Give the marble a gentle push. What happens?

3 Cut a triangle out of a second plate.

4 Repeat step 2 with the second plate. What happens this time? Compare the paint trails made by the marble.

WHAT'S GOING ON?

An object will go straight until something makes it turn. The curved edge of the plate makes the marble roll in a circle. When the marble gets to the break in the plate, it goes straight again.

05

BOOKS OF A FEATHER

WHAT YOU WILL NEED

two thick books that are the same size

DIRECTIONS

1   Open both books to the last page.

2   Place the last page of one book over the last page of the other book. Put the next page of the first book over the second book.

3   Keep **overlapping** the pages until you get to the front covers.

4   Try to pull the books apart.

5   Hold onto one of the books. Try to let the other book fall.

WHAT'S GOING ON?

The books won't pull apart. Each page is pressed against the other pages. This causes **friction**. Friction keeps the books together.

MYSTERY SCIENCE FRICTION

WHAT YOU WILL NEED

funnel

2 plastic bottles

uncooked rice

2 pencils

DIRECTIONS

1. Use the funnel to fill each bottle with rice. Fill them up to 1 inch (2.5 cm) from the top.

2. Put the cap on one bottle. Shake it. Take off the cap. The bottle looks full.

3. Tap the bottom of the other bottle on a hard surface. Push the rice down with your finger. Make room and fill with more rice. Repeat until you can't make room for any more rice.

4. Put a pencil in each bottle. Pull up on the pencils. What happens?

WHAT'S GOING ON?

There is more rice in the second bottle. The extra rice causes **friction**. The friction keeps the pencil from coming out. Instead, you pick the bottle up!

THE MAGIC RICE ELEVATOR

WHAT YOU WILL NEED

clay

jar with lid

uncooked rice

funnel

DIRECTIONS

① Roll the clay into a ball.

2   Place the ball gently on the bottom of the jar.

③ Using a funnel, fill the jar two-thirds full of rice. Make sure the clay ball is completely covered.

④ Screw the jar's lid on tightly. Shake the jar up and down. Continue shaking until the clay ball gets to the top of the rice.

WHAT'S GOING ON?

When you shake the jar, rice fills the space below the ball. The ball rises to the top, even though it is heavier than rice.

08

UNBELIEVABLE BALANCING ACT

WHAT YOU WILL NEED

drinking straw

toothpick

clay

ruler

DIRECTIONS

1. Fold the straw in half.

2. Push one tip of the toothpick through the fold in the straw.

3. Roll two small balls of clay. Make sure they are the same size.

4. Put a clay ball on each end of the straw.

5. Balance the end of the toothpick on your finger. Now try it on the edge of a table.

WHAT'S GOING ON?

Everything has a center of gravity. At the center, an object's weight is held up by one point. The toothpick is balancing the straw at its center of gravity.

FLOATING & FLYING BALLOON BOAT

WHAT YOU WILL NEED

large plastic tub

water

paper cup

scissors

hole punch

drinking straw

ruler

balloon

rubber band

clay

DIRECTIONS

1. Fill the tub with water. Cut off the top half of the paper cup. Punch a hole in the side of the cup near the bottom.

2. Cut a straw 2 inches (5 cm) long. Put one end into the balloon. Use the rubber band to hold it in place.

3. Put the balloon and straw inside the cup. Push the end of the straw out through the hole.

4. Seal the hole inside the cup with the clay. Blow up the balloon. Pinch the straw to keep the air in. Put the cup in the plastic tub. Let go.

WHAT'S GOING ON?

Every action has an opposite **reaction**. When air escapes the balloon, It pushes the balloon forward. The air goes one way. The balloon goes the opposite way!

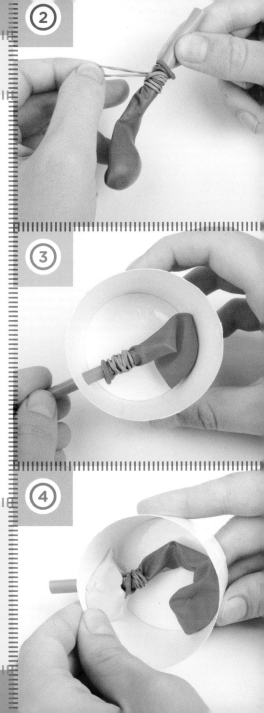

10 FLAT MARBLE GRAVITY DROP

WHAT YOU WILL NEED

card stock

pencil

ruler

scissors

clear tape

drinking glass

water

flat glass marble

DIRECTIONS

1   Draw a rectangle on the card stock. Make it 2 inches (5 cm) by 10 inches (25 cm). Cut it out.

2   Tape the short ends of the rectangle together. Now you have a paper ring.

3   Fill the glass with water. Balance the ring on the rim of the glass. Put the flat marble on top of the ring.

4   Stick the pencil through the ring. Move the pencil very fast to the left. It pulls the ring off the glass. What happens to the marble?

WHAT'S GOING ON?

The marble didn't stay on the ring. It fell into the glass. With the ring suddenly gone, gravity pulled the marble straight down.

11

ROUGH & SMOOTH FRICTION PULL

WHAT YOU WILL NEED

rubber band

scissors

small box

clear tape

marbles

cutting board

ruler

1 cup sugar

2 tablespoons liquid soap

measuring cups & spoons

DIRECTIONS

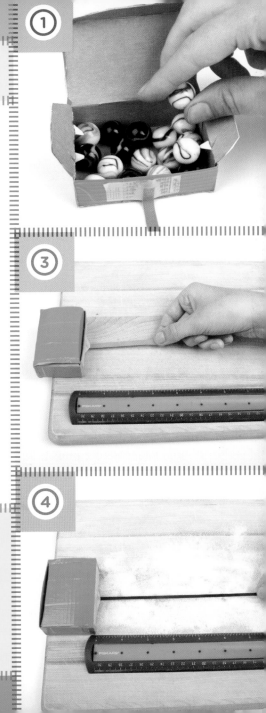

① Cut through the rubber band. Tape one end to the side of the box. Fill the box with marbles.

2 Place the box at one end of the cutting board.

③ Slowly pull on the rubber band. Measure how far it stretches before the box moves. Measure how far it stretches while the box moves.

④ Spread the sugar evenly over the cutting board. Repeat step 3.

5 Clean off the sugar. Spread the soap evenly on the cutting board. Repeat step 3.

WHAT'S GOING ON?

Rough surfaces have more **friction** than smooth ones. The sugar increases the friction between the box and board. So it's harder to pull the box. The soap reduces the friction. So it's easier to pull the box.

CONCLUSION

You just found out that science can be super simple! And you did it using gravity and motion. Keep your thinking cap on! What other experiments can you do with gravity and motion?

GLOSSARY

crumple – to crush or bend something out of shape.

friction – the resistance between two surfaces that are touching each other.

momentum – the force of something in motion caused by its mass and speed.

overlap – to make something lie partly on top of something else.

pendulum – something hanging from a single point so it can swing freely back and forth.

reaction – an action or movement of one force or object that is caused by the action or movement of another force or object.